PLAY PRESENT

A Mental Skills Training Program for Basketball Players

Graham H. Betchart, MA

Playbook design by Mary Teruel

PLAY PRESENT

A Mental Skills Training Program for Basketball Players

GRAHAM H. BETCHART, MA

80%

of the game is

Mental

"The mental part is the hardest part and I think that's the part that separates the good players from the great players."

Michael Jordan

Train
YOUR MIND

*"You always have to be on edge.
You always have to take every practice, every game, like it is your last."*

Kobe Bryant

Run
THE PLAYS

"You can make all the excuses you want, but if you're not mentally tough and you're not prepared to play every night, you're not going to win."

Larry Bird

Trust
The Process

THE GAME PLAN

How to run the plays and use this playbook.

"Your reputation will not win games. You must be ready mentally and physically."
Red Auerbach

1

Pre Game and Practice

Read the playbook.
Do MVP.

2

In Game and Practice

Play Present.
Play the Mental Game.

3

Post Game and Practice

Assess your Mental Game.
Learn and Let Go.

Play 1 WIN

What's Important Now

1 Pre Game and Practice

A You control believing in your talent and your abilities but you can't control winning, results, outcomes, other people, statistics, or the final score. Therefore the toughest defender and best competition you will ever face is **Yourself**. If you focus on who's going to win while you are playing, you have lost your focus and have made it harder for you to win. To win you have to get out of your own way and unlock your full potential with mental training.

B You control your process of relentlessly attacking, being aggressive and assertive, and trusting your skills in the present moment on the court—but you don't control the results of your process. You can't be in the moment and be thinking about winning at the same time. Your mind can only focus on one task at a time. Focus on the present play—and nothing else. If you try to multitask, you will lose.

C The irony of winning is that focusing on winning during the competition hurts your chances of success. Focus on what you do control. You control developing your champion mindset—which is your attitude, effort, focus, and actions in the here and now. Nobody can take your mindset from you but you can give it away. Don't try to be perfect at results. Free yourself from that restrictive mindset and be perfect at your process—because that is what you control. The process is the pleasure. The journey is the destination.

"I would tell players to relax and never think about what's at stake. Just think about the basketball game. If you start to think about who is going to win the championship, you've lost your focus."

Michael Jordan

Play 1 WIN

What's Important Now

"Don't let what you can't do interfere with what you can do."
John Wooden

2 In Game and Practice

WIN – Focus on What's Important Now
Control your actions in the present moment against the task at hand.

3 Post Game and Practice

Did you narrow your focus to only your actions in the present moment and compete only against the task at hand?

○ Some Plays? ○ Most Plays? ○ EVERY PLAY?

Play 2 Play Present

See Breathe Do

1 Pre Game and Practice

A You control competing against the play you see in front of you. You can't control the past or a future play. Your vision gets you into the present. When your mind wanders away from the task at hand, you no longer see what's in front of you. SEE.

B You control your focus at all times, and focusing on a deep slow breath will always bring you back into the present because your breath is happening right now. You can't compete against the last play or a future play. When your breathing is shallow and quick, your game feels tense and restricted. BREATHE.

C You control what you do at all times on the court, but you don't control how you feel. Trust your skills and allow your body to perform and do what it has been trained to do regardless of how you feel. Make your actions powerful and do your work, being aggressive, assertive, and attacking, on the court in the present. DO.

"If my mind wasn't in the present moment, the here and now, my body and energy wouldn't be, either. The present was something I could control, unlike those useless thoughts about a past or future situation that wasn't in my control at all."

Joe Montana

PLAY 2 Play Present

See Breathe Do

"In basketball — as in life — true joy comes from being fully present in each and every moment, not just when things are going your way. Of course, it's no accident that things are more likely to go your way when you stop worrying about whether you're going to win or lose and focus your full attention on what's happening right this moment."

Phil Jackson

2 In Game and Practice

See only what's on the court right now. Follow your breath. Take aggressive, assertive, and attacking action in the Here and Now.

3 Post Game and Practice

Did you take aggressive, assertive, and attacking action in the present using your eyes and your breath to keep you engaged and focused on the present?

- ❍ Some Plays?
- ❍ Most Plays?
- ❍ EVERY PLAY?

PLAY 3 Next Play Speed

Your ability to refocus quickly on the task at hand

1 Pre Game and Practice

A You will lose your focus during the game and you are in total control of refocusing fast onto the next play. This is called next play speed. It's not about forgetting about the last play – its about getting into the current play and back into the Here and Now.

B If you try to forget about the last play, you are actually focusing on it. The key to moving onto the next play in under one second is to SEE and engage in the play in front of you with your eyes, breath, and actions. You must be aware of when you have lost your focus. Pay attention to your attention.

C Playing present is challenging, so don't beat yourself up with negative self talk when you lose your focus. Calmly refocus with your eyes back to the task at hand. The faster you refocus on the next play, the better your results will be. Fail fast and move on.

"Whatever is in the past has already been done. I'm trying to do the best I can in the here and now. You've got to be present when you play."

Tiger Woods

PLAY 3 Next Play Speed

Your ability to refocus quickly on the task at hand

"Basketball is a complex dance that requires shifting from one objective to another at lightning speed. To excel, you need to act with a clear mind and be totally focused."

Phil Jackson

2 In Game and Practice

Refocus back to the present moment, back to competing against the task at hand fast after you have lost your focus.

3 Post Game and Practice

Did you refocus back to the present moment in under one second after you lost your focus?

○ Some Plays? ○ Most Plays? ○ EVERY PLAY?

REFOCUS

FAST

PLAY 4 Find Flow

You can play great no matter how you feel

1 Pre Game and Practice

A For 80 percent of your career you will not feel great. This is why the game is 80 percent mental. For 20 percent of your career you will feel great and be in flow or the zone. Everyone plays great when they feel great. Mastering the mental game is not about trying to feel great all the time on the court. It's about understanding how to find flow and get into your zone when you don't feel great. Being consistent on the court is about a consistent mindset because your feelings will vary from day to day and play to play. It's about having good bad days.

B You do not need to feel great to play great. You can feel all kinds of ways and still play great. Some games you will feel overly excited and energized, and your challenge will be to relax and be cool. Some games you will feel fatigued and fearful, and your challenge will be to act aggressive. Some games you will feel amazing, and your challenge will be to relentlessly attack and have no mercy on the competition.

C Your feelings don't need to dictate your actions or outcomes. You can always act how you choose on the court. You can act your way into the feeling. You must be aware of how you feel and make the right choice. You must act your way into the feeling. You will destruct and defeat yourself if you stay locked into a mindset that says you must feel great to play great.

"Mental toughness is really all about not getting too high or getting too low but just kind of staying pretty even-keeled… the trick is to not get too emotionally attached to the situation."

Kobe Bryant

Play 4 Find Flow

You can play great no matter how you feel

"You are in the presence of a true competitor when you observe that he or she is indeed getting the most joy out of the most difficult circumstances. ***The real competitors love a tough situation.*** *That is when they focus better and function better. Their competitive greatness."*

John Wooden

2 In Game and Practice

Fully accept your current state, compete to find flow, know you will be successful.

3 Post Game and Practice

Did you accept you current emotional state and compete to find flow regardless of how you felt?

❍ Some Plays? ❍ Most Plays? ❍ EVERY PLAY?

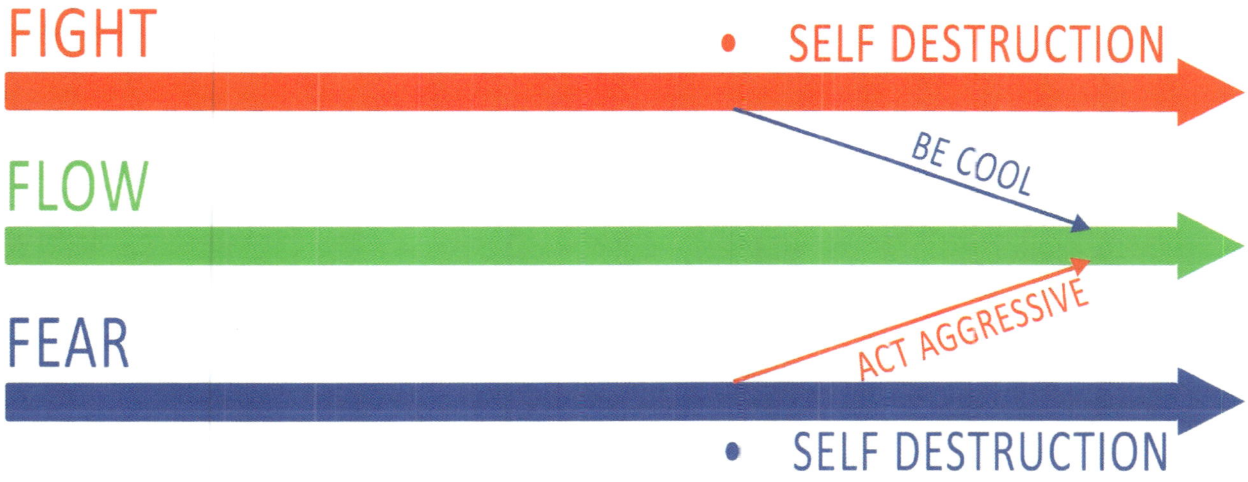

Play 5 See Breathe Be

From Fight to Flow

1 Pre Game and Practice

A Your greatest strength is also your great weakness if you don't learn to harness your power and use it to your advantage. Look at anger, frustration, and competitive fire as the color red. Too much red will destroy you. Finding flow is the key. When you feel 'red' and competitive your challenge is to Be Cool. The hardest thing to do when you are heated is be cool. It's easy to self-destruct and call it competitiveness. The real competition is within you and lies in being with your feelings and acting cool when you are overheated. Acting out is a self-prophecy that you will stop yourself.

B You can learn to relax while feeling extremely heated —you can be cool and feel frustrated at the same time. It's called being mindful. It means that you are in control of your actions and not reacting to how you feel in that moment. It starts with being aware of when you are not in your zone and you are too energized and agitated. This moment of awareness is the moment of truth. You now have the responsibility as the ultimate competitor to embrace the real challenge YOU and be cool when you feel like fighting. You must be with your feelings and be mindful. Acting how you feel is what animals do. Acting how you choose is what a mindful master competitor does. Own yourself and you own the game.

C The greatest action is no action sometimes. The greatest competition is in not acting sometimes. Impulse control is a choice. Your breath will cool you down and give you an action to take instead of acting out and self-destructing. You will be heated at times; this is guaranteed. Make the choice to be cool and simply be.

"The less tension and effort, the faster and more powerful you will be."

Bruce Lee

Play 5 See Breathe Be

From Fight to Flow

"What I tried to do was get them to walk away from confrontations and not let themselves be distracted. If somebody fouled them hard, I suggested turning around, take a deep breath, and staying as composed as possible so they could keep there minds on the goal."

Phil Jackson

2 In Game and Practice

Just breathe and be cool.

3 Post Game and Practice

Did you take a breath instead of acting impulsively. Were you mindful when you felt like fighting?

○ Some Plays? ○ Most Plays? ○ EVERY PLAY?

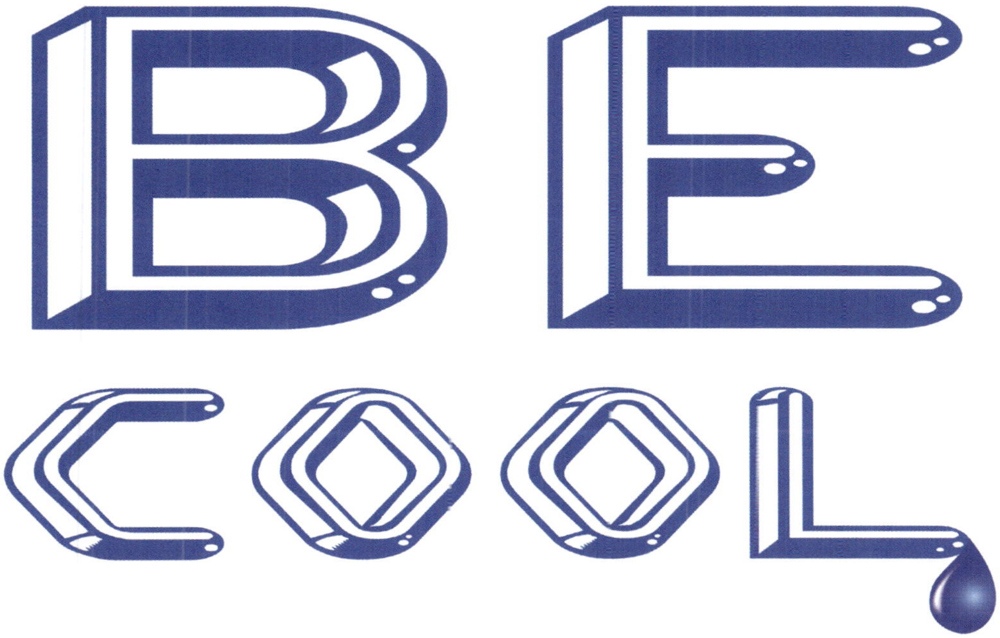

PLAY 6 See Breathe Do

Maintaining your Flow

1 Pre Game and Practice

A Sometimes the greatest challenge you will face is allowing yourself to dominate and be the best player on the court. When you have the ability and skills to do something on the court, you have the responsibility to use those skills and abilities every play ***everyday***. It's ok to be the best player on the court and to dominate the game. Do not be afraid of your success because it is your right to be as successful as you are capable of being.

B When you have the green light on the court you do not have to ask for permission to Do Work. Take what's yours because nobody will ever give it to you. However, when you are feeling it, you do not have to be overly aggressive. You are already in the flow state, so now you have to observe your performance and let it happen. You don't have to rush anything and try to win the game in one possession or score all your points in one play. The game is a marathon, so play it one play at a time and savor each moment as your personal masterpiece, and enjoy the zone and being in flow.

C When you are humble with your success you are now playing the art of war you are keeping your enemies close. It's ok to be as good as you are capable of being —that's your job and birthright. When you combine being a dominant and relentlessly savage competitor with being grateful for your talent, humble, and appreciative of those who have helped you and play with you by your side and against you in competition —you become invincible. Don't give your opponents fuel for motivation. Humble is hard.

"Effort within the mind further limits the mind, because effort implies struggle towards a goal and when you have a goal, a purpose, an end in view, you have placed a limit on the mind."

Bruce Lee

Play 6 See Breathe Do

Maintaining your Flow

"The key is seeing and doing. If you're focusing on anything other than reading the court and doing what needs to be done, the moment will pass you by."

Phil Jackson

2 In Game and Practice

Observe your performance, let it happen and enjoy the experience.

3 Post Game and Practice

Did you observe your performance and enjoy every moment of being in the zone?

○ Some Plays? ○ Most Plays? ○ EVERY PLAY?

DO
WORK

Play 7 See Breathe Act

From Fear to Flow

1 Pre Game and Practice

A Some days the greatest challenge will be your feelings of fatigue and fear. You must be mindful here and coach yourself. Feeling fear on the court does not mean you are in any danger at all. Fear is only a feeling and it is not based in reality most of the time. There is a difference between being in actual danger and the feeling of fear. You can feel fear and play your game as if you are in your zone. Fear is an opportunity to excel and reach new levels. The feelings are real, but being in danger is not real. Be mindful.

B Feeling fatigue does not mean your body can't perform. You are in control of how you act when you feel fatigue. Being a mindful competitor or conscious baller means that you recognize when you feel fear and fatigue but you choose to play your game anyway. Courage allows you to deal with fear.

C You are in control of feeling the fear. There is no such thing as being fearless. Everyone feels fear but the great athletes reframe the feeling of fear into an opportunity to rise. They call *fear joy*. This is being mindful. This is being proactive instead of reactive.

"To hell with circumstances; I create opportunities."

Bruce Lee

Play 7 See Breathe Act

From Fear to Flow

"A leaders most powerful ally is his or her own example. Leaders don't just talk about doing something; they do it."
John Wooden

2 In Game and Practice

Feel fear and passive but act aggressive and assertive.

3 Post Game and Practice

Did you stay on attack mode, acting aggressive and assertive when you felt fearful and passive?

- ❍ Some Plays? ❍ Most Plays? ❍ EVERY PLAY?

ACT AGGRESSIVE

Play 8 MVP

Meditation, Visualization, Positive Affirmation

1 Pre Game and Practice

A Meditation

Start to breathe in through your nose and out through your mouth. Feel the air come in through your nose, fill your belly, and slowly exit through your mouth. Feel your breath and learn to focus on the moment. Let the day's distractions leave with each exhale. Notice thoughts that come up, and return your focus to your breath. Do not judge yourself when your focus goes to your thoughts simply observe them like passing clouds and watch them drift away as you refocus on your breath. Sense everything that is happening in the moment. Bring out your sensing mind and let your thinking mind go. Get to the here and now. Breathe.

"I meditated with the team before games."
Kobe Bryant

B Visualization

Using all of your senses, visualize, imagine, feel, or pretend either watching yourself or being yourself playing successfully executing the game plan, overcoming challenges, finishing strong, shooting and making plays with confidence, playing strong defense, playing your game, attacking assertively and aggressively, staying in the moment, and constantly moving on to the next play.

"I always visualized my success… Seeing success before it happened put me in a positive frame of mind and prepared me to play the game."
Michael Jordan

C Positive Affirmations

Repeat strong motivational affirmations that affirm your self-image, your abilities and talents. Example: *"I See, Breathe, Do. I am capable of all things when I play present."*

"It's the repetition of affirmations that leads to belief. And once that belief becomes a deep conviction, things begin to happen."
Muhammad Ali

Play 8 MVP

Meditation, Visualization, Positive Affirmation

"Victorious warriors win first and then go to war, while defeated warriors go to war first and then seek to win."
Sun Tzu

2 In Game and Practice

Play present.

3 Post Game and Practice

Did you do MVP?

○ Yes ○ No

PLAY 9 The Next Level

Comfortable Being Uncomfortable

1 Pre Game and Practice

A If you stay still and stagnant you will destruct because the level you are at is not stable and not permanent. It's an illusion that will burn away soon. You must always be growing. You will never outperform your own self-image. You must see yourself as a player who is destined for success if you want success for yourself. If you want to get to the next level in your career you have to expect yourself and see yourself getting to the next level. There is no safety net when you are changing levels.

B Strengthening your mind feels the same as strengthening your body; uncomfortable. Getting to the next level requires getting really uncomfortable and that's ok. Growing hurts, and when you resist being uncomfortable mentally, you are resisting getting to the next level. The next level requires that you get uncomfortable.

C Getting to the next level mentally means getting out of your comfort zone willingly and establishing a new self-image with new ways of acting and thinking. Go right into the fire and you will realize that you have what it takes. Stay where you are and you will destruct. You must always be growing. Always growing is about never being comfortable staying at the level you are at.

"He who is not courageous enough to take risks will accomplish nothing in life."
Muhammad Ali

PLAY 9 The Next Level

Comfortable Being Uncomfortable

"In the middle of difficulty, lies opportunity."
Albert Einstein

2 In Game and Practice

Put yourself in uncomfortable situations.

3 Post Game and Practice

Do you allow yourself to be comfortable being uncomfortable ?

- ❍ Some Days? ❍ Most Days? ❍ EVERY DAY?

PLAY 10 Greatness

Reframing Failure as Necessary for Success

1 Pre Game and Practice

A You have to fail to become great. Greatness requires that you fail first. You must fail to win. Put all your energy and focus into playing to play great. As soon as you start to play to not make any mistakes or to not fail YOU ARE DONE and have made the biggest failure of all.

B Michael Jordan has missed more shots than anyone in the history of the NBA during the regular season and Kobe Bryant has missed more shots in the regular season and playoffs combined than anyone in the history of the NBA. What if their mindset was to not miss any shots and not make mistakes. They would have been frozen and never reached the levels they have reached in the game. Greatness is about learning to reframe how you judge success. If you trust your shot and take it but it doesn't go in that's a success not a failure. Be proud of your miss as it is getting you closer to success.

C When you play to avoid failure or mistakes, you avoid success and becoming great at the same time. When you understand that your mistakes and failures are a necessary part of success you don't see them as failures. When you are focused on growing, you see mistakes and failures as opportunities to grow and learn. Be proud of making mistakes and persevering. Fail fast and fail to the top. It's all a mindset. It's called the growth mindset.

"I've missed more than 9000 shots in my career. I've lost almost 300 games. Twenty-six times, I've been trusted to take the game winning shot and missed. I've failed over and over and over again in my life. And that is why I succeed."

Michael Jordan

Play 10 Greatness

Reframing Failure as Necessary for Success

"I can't stand a ballplayer who plays in fear. Any fellow who has a good shot has got to take it and keep taking it. So he misses — so what?"
Red Auerbach

2 In Game and Practice

Play to play great – not to avoid failure. Put ALL your energy into playing to play great.

3 Post Game and Practice

Did you play to play great, reframing failure as the key to success?

○ Some Plays? ○ Most Plays? ○ EVERY PLAY?

Play 11 Mastery

Play Present - Practice Present - Live Present

1 Pre Game and Practice

A Repetition of your mindset creates retention of your mindset. Working on your mental game is like working on your shot. You have to practice and train daily. There is no quick fix with mental training. There is no overnight success. Your commitment and training will be tested all the time. Put in the work play after play, day after day, and season after season. Eventually people will say you have a motor, but we will know that you have a trained mindset built for success.

B Your most powerful weapon, your mind, can only be sharpened through trials and tribulations. The only path to becoming a conscious baller is through the fire and into the storm. When you can relax in the middle of the storm you are in control. This happens when your mind is sharpened from years of refining and developing your craft of the game of basketball, your life's work. To create your mental spear you must be brave and allow yourself to be vulnerable, as this leads to victory in the mental game.

C Ultimately you have to have success off the court to even have a chance to have success on the court. There would be no point in only using these mental skills to excel on the basketball court. These are life skills and basketball is the medium we love and dedicate our lives to. Playing fully present is your mission on the court and living fully present is your mission in life. Whereever you are with your body, be there with your mind as well—this is living fully engaged – this is conscious balling.

"The key to success is to keep growing in all areas of life—mental, emotional, spiritual, as well as physical."

Julius Erving

PLAY 11 Mastery

Play Present - Practice Present - Live Present

"If people knew how hard I worked to get my mastery, it wouldn't seem so wonderful at all."
Michelangelo

2 In Game and Practice

Sharpen your mind on and off the court.

3 Post Game and Practice

Do you use your mental skills to play present, practice present and live present?

❍ Some Days? ❍ Most Days? ❍ EVERY DAY?

Play PRESENT

"The important thing to remember is it's not about how much you practice...
but how much your mind is present during practice."

Kobe Bryant

THE Competition

YOU

"Know yourself and you will win all battles."
Sun Tzu

Play
THE MENTAL GAME

"Your mind is what makes everything work."
Kareem Abdul Jabar

The Mental Game

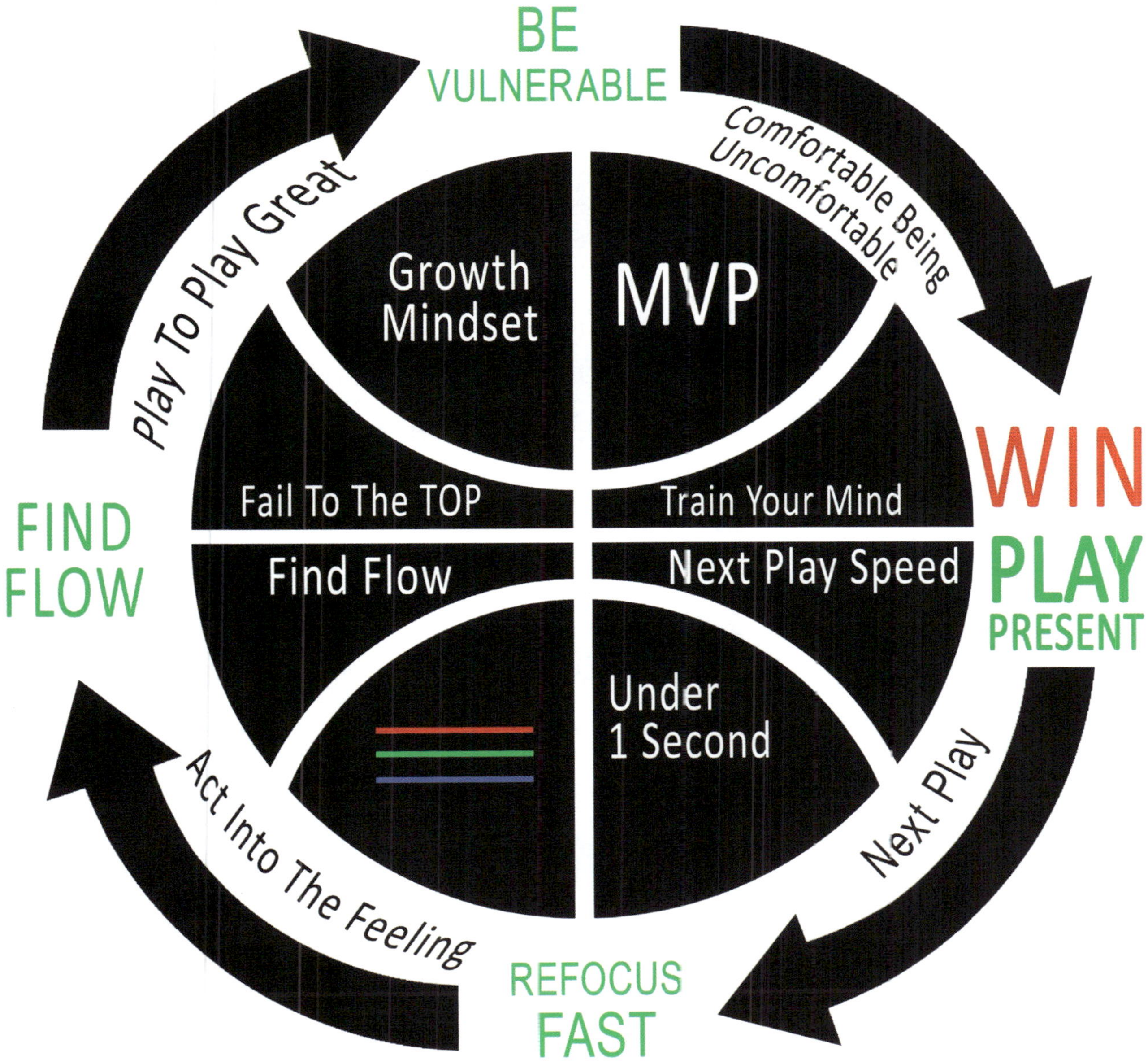

Follow Green To Win

The Foundation

"A man is not great because he hasn't failed; a man is great because failure hasn't stopped him."
Confucius

Be Courageous

To go all in, run the plays and play the mental game

Be Compassionate

To live with the results

Be Competitive

To run the plays until the plays run themselves

The Realization

"We are what we repeatedly do. Excellence, then, is not an act but a habit."
Aristotle

Focus is a Choice.

Confidence is an Action.

Greatness is a Decision.

FOCUS

"The successful warrior is the average man, with laser-like focus."

Bruce Lee

CONCENTRATE

"Concentration and mental toughness are the margins of victory."

Bill Russell

BELIEVE

"People have always doubted whether I was good enough to play this game at this level. I thought I was, and I thought I could be. What other people thought was really always irrelevant to me."

Steve Nash

Win THE MENTAL GAME

YOU ARE
UNSTOPPABLE

My name is Graham Betchart and I am the co-founder of Play Present, a Mental Skills Training Firm for basketball players. I am a Mental Skills Coach for basketball players and I have trained numerous professional, collegiate, and prep players.

I designed this Mental Skills Training program specifically for you, the basketball player. This program is designed to be practiced daily just like any other basketball skill.

Do not read this once and put it away.

Bring it with you to every practice and every game.

Read it every day if you are truly competitive and want to be the best.

80% of your game is dependent upon how serious you are about training your mind, developing a winning mindset, and building real lasting supreme confidence.

playpresent.com

44744481R00030

Made in the USA
Lexington, KY
08 September 2015